Schedule C
Tax Deductions
Revealed

*The Plain English Guide to
101 Self-Employed Tax Breaks
(For Sole Proprietors Only)*

Small Business Tax Tips, Volume 2

Wayne Davies, EA

Copyright © 2016 by Wayne Davies

Get 3 Free Tax-Saving Gifts at
SelfEmployedTaxDeductionsToday.com

**#1: Tax-Saving Guide for Small Businesses
#2: Small Business Tax Tips Newsletter
#3: $150 Worth of Tax Coupons**

SCHEDULE C TAX DEDUCTIONS REVEALED

TABLE OF CONTENTS

3 Free Gifts 5

What People Are Saying About Wayne Davies............................ 7

Why You Should **Not** Read This Book.. 10

Why I Wrote This Book.. 12

Chapter 1. Are You a Sole Proprietor . . . And Don't Even Know It?.. 16

Chapter 2. The Easy Part of Schedule C...................................... 19

Chapter 3. Schedule C, Lines 1-7 (Part 1)................................... 22

Chapter 4. Schedule C, Lines 1-7 (Part 2)................................... 24

Chapter 5. How to Deduct Advertising Expense on Schedule C, Line 8.. 27

Chapter 6. How to Deduct Actual Vehicle Expenses on Schedule C, Line 9.. 29

Chapter 7. How to Deduct Vehicle Mileage Expense on Schedule C, Line 9.. 31

Chapter 8. How to Deduct Commissions and Fees on Schedule C, Line 10... 33

Chapter 9. How to Deduct Contract Labor on Schedule C, Line 11 35

Chapter 10. How to Deduct Business Equipment on Schedule C, Line 13.. 37

Chapter 11. How to Deduct Employee Benefits On Schedule C, Line 14 41

Chapter 12. How to Deduct Insurance on Schedule C, Line 15 44

Chapter 13. How to Deduct Interest on Schedule C, Line 16.. 46

Chapter 14. How to Deduct Legal & Professional Services on Schedule C, Line 17 48

Chapter 15. How to Deduct Office Expenses on Schedule C, Line 18 50

Chapter 16. How to Deduct Retirement Plan Expense on Schedule C, Line 19 52

Chapter 17. How to Deduct Rent & Lease Expense on Schedule C, Line 20 54

Chapter 18. How to Deduct Repairs and Maintenance Expense on Schedule C, Line 21 56

Chapter 19. How to Deduct Supplies on Schedule C, Line 22 58

Chapter 20. How to Deduct Taxes on Schedule C, Line 23 60

Chapter 21. How to Deduct Travel Expenses on Schedule C, Line 24a 62

Chapter 22. How to Deduct Meals Expenses on Schedule C, Line 24b 65

Chapter 23. How to Deduct Utilities on Schedule C, Line 25.. 67

Chapter 24. How to Deduct Wages on Schedule C, Line 26 (Part 1) 69

Chapter 25. How to Deduct Wages on Schedule C, Line 26 (Part 2) 72

Chapter 26. How to Deduct Miscellaneous Expenses on Schedule C, Line 27 74

Chapter 27. How to Prepare Schedule C, Lines 33-42, Cost of Goods Sold (Part 1) 76

Chapter 28. How to Prepare Schedule C, Lines 33-42, Cost of Goods Sold (Part 2) 79

Chapter 29. How to Prepare Schedule C, Lines 43-47 82

Chapter 30. Other Tax Forms That You May Be Required To File 84

Chapter 31. Home Office Deduction 86

Chapter 32. 101 Deductions 89

Chapter 33. Now What? 96

Recommended Resources 97

About The Author 102

One Last Thing 103

THE PLAIN ENGLISH GUIDE TO 101 SELF-EMPLOYED TAX BREAKS

3 FREE GIFTS

As my way of saying "Thank you!" for reading this book, I've included these special bonuses for you. To get all 3 gifts visit

<u>www.SelfEmployedTaxDeductionsToday.com</u>

GIFT #1 - Tax-Saving Report
You'll receive Free Instant Access to my Tax-Saving Guide:

"Top 10 Tax Deductions . . .
For Small Business Owners & Self-Employed People"

GIFT #2 - Tax Tips Newsletter
When you request my Tax-Saving Guide (above), you'll also get a free subscription to my Tax Newsletter. You'll receive easy-to-understand tax tips delivered to your inbox weekly.

GIFT #3 - Tax Coupons Worth $150
These coupons include a 30-minute phone consultation with me and a confidential review of your most recently filed income tax returns (business and personal), at no charge.

Why am I doing this? Because taxes are complicated, convoluted and confusing (not to mention costly)! And I've done my best to simplify them for you in this book.

SCHEDULE C TAX DEDUCTIONS REVEALED

Maybe you'll read this book and say, "Oh, yeah. I understand this stuff! It makes perfect sense." And you'll know exactly what to do to utilize the many deductions explained here.

It is also possible that you'll read this book and say, "I think I get it. But I sure would like to ask a question or two for clarification, to make sure I understand how to apply a specific tax deduction to my particular situation."

That's why I'm giving you these coupons:

Coupon #1 – Free 30-minute phone consultation. You get to talk with me and ask me any questions you have about the tax deductions explained in this book, in case you need clarification or just want to make sure you understand how to apply them to your particular situation.

Coupon #2 – Free review of your most recently filed tax returns (Business and Personal). I'll take a look at your tax situation and let you know if there are any deductions you've overlooked, and I can also tell you the tax savings you'll get by putting these tax deductions to work.

To access the coupons immediately, visit
www.selfemployedtaxdeductionstoday.com/tax-coupons.pdf

To get the other 2 gifts today, visit
www.SelfEmployedTaxDeductionsToday.com

THE PLAIN ENGLISH GUIDE TO 101 SELF-EMPLOYED TAX BREAKS

WHAT PEOPLE ARE SAYING ABOUT WAYNE DAVIES

"You are a wealth of information. Keep it coming!"
-- Carlos Rivera

"Thank you for the great tax-saving strategies you've helped me to use in my business. During that one 30-minute phone call, you made one simple suggestion that saved me $2,295 in taxes. I never would have thought of this strategy on my own. I've been able to utilize this same technique again and again -- and this year I'll save over $6,000 from this one loophole."
-- Gary Ritter

"Over the past year, Wayne has found and made recommendations that have resulted in some very real tax savings. I take pride in understanding many accounting principles and a healthy measure of tax law. However, Wayne saved us $3,700 this year with two simple suggestions. I wasn't aware of one of them; the other I didn't think of, and I wouldn't have until too late. We've been with Wayne just a year, and he has called with those two suggestions. I don't recall our previous accountant coming up with anything, in almost three years."
-- Dennis Malott

"I just wanted to drop a quick note of thanks for all of your help to minimize taxes. In such a complicated tax world, you showed me how to save $2,000 in taxes on just one tax

SCHEDULE C TAX DEDUCTIONS REVEALED

strategy alone. No other tax professional has taken the time to show these tax savings opportunities for my company. Your services have been professional and timely, and also articulate and accurate - a very important facet of your business. It's nice to know that I can run my business and not have to worry about the "tax" side of my business. I look forward to learning more strategies for tax savings in the future. Keep up the great job!"
-- Ron Schmucker

"Having been associated over 20 years now, I feel privileged that we've crossed paths. Since then you have demonstrated that you genuinely care about the success of my business resulting in our personal gain. You have shown us ways to save taxes in which we were unaware of, through different vehicles offered by the government. Through these years, we have quickly developed a rapport, and we have become friends during our business relationship. Wayne, thanks for your help over the years."
-- Bernie Place

"Just a note to thank you, and express our appreciation for the reliable work you do for us. Your willingness to go the extra mile in doing research and answering our many questions thoroughly has been greatly appreciated. It puts our minds at ease to know we can depend on you to have our taxes done before the deadlines!"
-- Loyal & Ann Mast

"I just wanted to write you a note to thank you for your tax saving suggestions that saved me $1,281 on my taxes last year. It sure was worth the few minutes we took to review

my tax situation. I also wanted to thank you for advising me on rolling my previous 401(k) account into an IRA account. This decision has enabled me to double my money in less than 5 years. I will be sure to recommend you to anyone who needs a great accountant."
-- Jeffery A. Rife

"Thank you for the competent, professional service you have rendered the last couple years. I am most pleased with your supervising and finalizing our corporate books of account and completing our corporate and my personal year-end income tax returns. Your advice and support regarding our Quickbooks software has been an extra bonus. We rest easier knowing we have an expert computer back-up a local phone call away."
-- Larry Lee

SCHEDULE C TAX DEDUCTIONS REVEALED

WHY YOU SHOULD **NOT** READ THIS BOOK

There are three reasons why you should not read this book.

REASON #1

If you're looking for an exhaustive in-depth explanation of every tax deduction under the sun, this book is not for you. There are other books that go into much more detail than this one.

My guess is that you don't have a lot of time to read about our crazy tax laws. Who does?

My goal is to give you a brief yet thorough explanation of the most common deductions a sole proprietor can claim on Schedule C. Fair enough?

REASON #2

If you are looking for illegal tax deductions, this book is not for you. Every deduction presented in this book is legitimate. If you want to get around the law by breaking the law, I cannot help you.

There are plenty of legal tax deductions. Why play around with funny money?

REASON #3

If you have this naive idea that a profitable sole proprietorship can pay zero taxes, this book is not for you. If your small business or self-employment activity is making money, you're going to pay some taxes. And generally speaking, the more money you make, the more taxes you pay.

But it is also very likely that if you are profitable, you can legally reduce your taxes. How much? That depends on several factors, such as how much profit you're making and what type of records you keep to track your deductions, and so forth.

The point here is this: don't expect to read this book and then magically have everything you need to know to suddenly pay no taxes at all. That is an unrealistic expectation.

Nuff said about that.

Let's get started!

Why I Wrote This Book

I wrote this book to answer the world's most frequently asked tax question.

Do you know what that is?

Here it is: "What's deductible?"

That's it. Without a doubt, it's the most common tax question I get every year. It comes in several forms, such as:

How do I identify all the deductions I'm allowed to take?
What deductions am I missing?
How do I make sure I'm taking all legal tax deductions?
Is there one resource that describes all deductions, A to Z?

Knowing all allowable Schedule C tax deductions is no easy task. Our beloved politicians have done much to complicate our lives in this regard.

Any long journey begins with a single step, so here's where you can start learning what's deductible: your income tax return. Go to the IRS website right now and print out a copy of Schedule C and take a close look. Here you'll find a list of about twenty deductible business expenses.

To get a current copy of the 2015 Schedule C, go here:

http://www.irs.gov/pub/irs-pdf/f1040sc.pdf

Schedule C is divided into five sections (Parts I-V). Part I is labeled "Income" and Part II is labelled "Expenses." So you'd think we should dive into Part II. But if you sell a product, we

THE PLAIN ENGLISH GUIDE TO 101 SELF-EMPLOYED TAX BREAKS

need to take a close look at Part I because this is where you deduct what's known as "Cost of Goods Sold" on Line 4.

For retailers, this is probably your largest expense. You get to deduct the wholesale cost of all products sold during the year. Part III of Schedule C (Lines 33 through 42) contains the details of how this expense is calculated, and the amount from Line 42 is transferred back to Line 4.

So that's your first and potentially biggest deduction, if you sell a product.

Now let's move on to Part II, Expenses. Take a good look at Lines 8-27. This section of Schedule C is a literal goldmine of deductions in alphabetical order. Here they are, with the corresponding Schedule C line number:

8-Advertising

9-Car and truck expenses

10-Commissions and fees

11-Contract labor

12-Depletion (OK, there's a rare one)

13-Depreciation and Section 179 deduction

14-Employee benefit programs

15-Insurance

16-Interest

17-Legal and professional services

SCHEDULE C TAX DEDUCTIONS REVEALED

18-Office expense

19-Pension and profit-sharing plans

20-Rent or lease

21-Repairs and maintenance

22-Supplies

23-Taxes and licenses

24a-Travel

24b-Meals and entertainment

25-Utilities

26-Wages (if you have employees)

27-Other expenses

Take special note of that last expense, Line 27, "Other expenses." That's my favorite! This is where you can deduct any other legitimate business expense that is not included on the lines 8-26. In fact, Part V is devoted exclusively to this "Other Expense" category. You can have any number of business expenses listed here, which are added together on Line 48 and then transferred back to Line 27.

Here's the deal. The purpose of this book is to take you line by line through Schedule C and explain each of these deductible expenses. This is not rocket science. But it is taxes. As you know, a little knowledge is powerful and can take you a long way from where you are now.

For example, how about Line 15 – Insurance. What goes there? There are many types of insurance: health insurance, car insurance, business liability insurance, renter's insurance, homeowner's insurance, life insurance, worker's compensation insurance. And so on. Do the premiums for all those types of insurance get reported here? Hmm. Good question!

See what I mean?

I'm going to answer the question "What's Deductible" with Plain English explanations of each line of Schedule C. I'm going to assume that you know very little (or nothing at all) about each of these deductions. I want you to understand the basics of deductible business expenses for the typical self-employed person. The more deductions you know about, the more deductions you'll be able to take. And the more deductions you take, the less tax you'll pay.

Does that sound like a good thing? Great! Let's keep moving.

Chapter 1. Are You a Sole Proprietor . . . And Don't Even Know It?

Do you wonder whether the IRS views you as a sole proprietor? Then you came to the right place. Step right up and get an answer to this all-important question.

According to the IRS, a sole proprietor is someone who owns an unincorporated business by himself/herself. There are two key words in that definition. Let's unpack them both.

First, "unincorporated." The IRS is saying that if your business is **not** a corporation, a partnership, or a limited liability company (LLC) that is taxed as a corporation or partnership, then you are a sole proprietor.

(Note: A single-owner LLC can be taxed like a sole proprietorship. Or it can be taxed like a corporation. It's up to the owner. If you do nothing, by default a single-owner LLC will be considered a sole proprietorship for tax purposes. To be taxed like a corporation, a LLC must tell the IRS via Form 8832, Entity Classification Election.)

Second, "business." If you are engaging in an activity such as selling a product or service with the intent to make a profit, then you own a business. The key word in that previous sentence is "intent," because you are not required to make a profit to have a business. You simply must have a profit motive and you must demonstrate that motive by doing things to further the interests of the business.

THE PLAIN ENGLISH GUIDE TO 101 SELF-EMPLOYED TAX BREAKS

And it doesn't necessarily matter how much time you spend in the pursuit of profit. You may have a regular full-time job as an employee for which you receive a W-2, and have a part-time business on the side. And as far as the IRS is concerned, a part-time business is a business.

The phrase "sole proprietor" has several well-known synonyms, such as "independent contractor" and "self-employed." These terms are used interchangeably and you'll find them used as such in business books as well as IRS publications.

Why is this such an important issue? With the explosion in recent years of online money-making opportunities like eBay and affiliate marketing, many people now meet the IRS definition of a sole proprietor and don't even realize it! I know that may sound hard to believe, but it's true.

Of course, there have always been plenty of home-based, part-time, small business opportunities for people eager to make some extra money. Think "moonlighting." Think Amway and multi-level marketing. Do those words ring any bells?

But the internet has given people a whole new range of money-making ideas. So if you are selling used items on eBay, you are considered a sole proprietor in the eyes the IRS, and you are required to report that income on your personal income tax return (assuming that you have not formed a corporation, partnership or LLC that is taxed like a corporation).

And by reporting the income and expenses from your fledgling online business, you have just significantly increased the complexity of your tax return. Congratulations, you are about to entered the wild and wacky world of small business taxes!

There are two things you can do to educate yourself on the basics of filing a tax return for your new small business. First, find a local tax professional who is experienced in preparing sole proprietorship returns. Do yourself a favor and don't try to do it yourself. And second, do some reading on the subject. I'm assuming that's why you have this book in your hands! I commend you for taking time to learn more. You don't have to become a small business tax expert, but you do have to understand the basics, and that's what this book is designed to do for you.

Chapter 2. The Easy Part of Schedule C

Are you a Sole Proprietor who faces the daunting task of filling out Schedule C every year? If you break out into a sweat just thinking about it, relax.

To get the most out of this chapter (and the rest of this book), have a copy of Schedule C in front of you as you read on. You can open up your tax return software program to Schedule C, download a copy from the IRS website, or use the printed paper version from a recently filed return.

Schedule C does have a few tricky parts, but it starts out nice and easy. Let's take a look at the section at the very top of the page, what I call "The Easy Part."

Name of proprietor – this should be your full legal personal name in the same format as it appears on Form 1040, Page 1. Important: Do not put your business name here; that goes on Line C.

Social security number – make sure this matches your Form 1040 info.

Next comes information that is labeled alphabetically from A to H.

A – Principal business or profession, including product or service.

Use a brief description of the business activity, such as "pest control" or "retail store" or "consultant".

SCHEDULE C TAX DEDUCTIONS REVEALED

B – Enter code from instructions.

This is a numeric code for your particular business. Refer to the chart in the Schedule C instructions to find the right code for your business. If you are using a software program, this chart is likely built right into the program.

C – Business name.

If you have one, put that in here. If you don't have a separate business name, which is quite common among self-employed people, leave this line blank.

D – Employer ID number.

If you have employees, you should have an Employer ID number, aka the Federal ID number. But it you don't have employees, you probably don't have an Employer ID (which is OK); if that's the case, leave this blank.

E – Business address.

If you have a business address that is different than the home address listed on Form 1040, Page 1, put that here. Otherwise, just use your home address.

F – Accounting method.

There are three choices: Cash, Accrual, and Other. Most Sole Proprietors use the Cash method, which means that you report income when it is received and you report expenses when they are paid. The Accrual method means that you report income when you have earned the right to receive it, regardless of when it is actually received; and you report expenses when you are obligated to pay them, regardless of when you actually pay them. The "Other" method is used by those who do a combination of both Cash and Accrual. If you are not sure which method to pick, you can read up on this in the Schedule C instructions or consult a tax professional. Plus I'll be addressing this issue later on, in Chapters 3 and 4.

G – Did you "materially participate" in the operation of this business during the year?

If you were involved in the business, check "Yes." If not, check "No."

H – Another question: If you started or acquired this business during the year, check the box. That's a pretty easy question to answer – in other words, is this the first year for this Sole Proprietorship? If so, check the box. If not, leave it blank.

I – Did you make any payments during the year that would require you to file Form(s) 1099. The purpose of this question is mainly to find out if you should have filed Form 1099-MISC for independent contractors. If you paid any independent contractors at least $600 during the year, you should be sending a Form 1099-MISC to those contractors and also filing a copy with the IRS. This is one way the IRS can track the income of other sole proprietors.

J – If "Yes," did you or will you file required Forms 1099?

This question goes with Question I. So if you answered "Yes" to Question I, now you must indicate whether you have already filed the required 1099's or intend to do so.

Chapter 3. Schedule C, Lines 1-7 (Part 1)

OK, get out a copy of Schedule C and let's take a look at Part I -- Income.

The purpose of Part I is to report your income, aka "sales" or "revenue." In other words, how much money did you make during the year from the sale of products and/or services?

Service-based businesses.

If your business sells a service but not a product, you've got it easy. The only line you will fill out in Part I is Line 1, Gross receipts or sales.

The one critical question you must know the answer to in order to correctly report income from services is this: do you use the Cash method or the Accrual method of accounting? Simply look up to Line F and see which box you checked.

If you use the Cash method, then you should report all income that customers/clients actually paid you in the current year. So if you did some work in December but have yet to receive payment as of December 31, you will not include that in the current year annual sales total. Assuming you get paid for that work in January, you will report that payment as income on the next year's return.

If you use the Accrual method, you must report all income for work you've done and invoiced in the current year, regardless of whether you've been paid for it by December 31.

If all your income comes from the sale of services, you will put your annual sales total on Line 1 and you are done with Part I. Lines 2-6 will have zeroes and Line 7 will be the same as Line 1. Easy enough?

Product-based businesses.

If you sell a product, you've got more work to do in Part I than a service-only business. After putting your total product sales amount in Line 1, you've also got to put amounts in Lines 2-5 as follows:

Line 2 – Returns and allowances. Any product returns must be reported here.

Line 3 – Subtract Line 2 from line 1 and put the difference on Line 3.

Line 4 – Cost of Goods Sold. This amount will come from Line 42 on Schedule C, Page 2, which is the section of Schedule C known as Part III, Cost of Goods Sold. So you must complete Part III before you can put a number in Line 4. So go over to Part III and complete Lines 33-42; then take the total from Line 42 and transfer it to Line 4.

Line 5 – Gross profit. Subtract Line 4 from Line 3 and put the difference in Line 5. "Gross profit" is the amount of profit you made from the sale of your products.

Chapter 4. Schedule C, Lines 1-7 (Part 2)

How did it go reading that last chapter?

At the risk of being a bit redundant, I'd like to continue our discussion of Schedule C, Line 1-7 and explain again the difference between the Cash Method and the Accrual Method of income reporting.

I realize that accounting lingo can be confusing. Perhaps you've been confused about how to report income on Schedule C. This chapter will help you get un-confused. I'm also going to focus on Sole Proprietors who sell services.

Let's define what we mean by "income". Generally speaking, income is the money you earned from the sale of products or services in your small business or self-employment activity. It is also called "gross receipts," "revenue," or "sales" and is typically reported on Schedule C, Line 1.

The key to knowing how to report your income is determined by your "Accounting Method". Take a look at the top of page 1 of Schedule C, right below your business name, address and other basic information. See Line F? It's labeled "Accounting Method" and you have three choices: Cash, Accrual and Other.

Most sole proprietors use the Cash method of accounting or the Accrual method of accounting, and it's critical that you understand the difference, especially when it comes to reporting your business income.

Here's a basic explanation of these two Accounting Methods for service businesses:

Cash Method.

This means that you report the income in the year you actually receive the money from your customer or client, regardless of when you provided the service.

Example #1: You provide a service to Mr. Client in December 2015 and he pays you in December 2015. You must report the income on your 2015 Schedule C.

Example #2: You provide a service to Mr. Client in December 2015 but he pays you in January 2016. You must report the income on your 2016 Schedule C.

Accrual Method.

This means that you report the income in the year that you invoice the customer or client, regardless of when payment is received.

Example #1: You provide a service to Mr. Client and send him an invoice in December 2015. Regardless of whether he pays you in 2015 or 2016, you must report the income from that invoice on the 2015 Schedule C (even if he pays you in 2016).

To summarize: Under the Cash Method, you report sales in the year you get paid. Under the Accrual Method, you report sales in the year you provide the service and bill the client, regardless of what year you get paid.

Now comes the obvious question: which method should you use? If you've been in business for a while, simply look at your Schedule C, Line F from last year and see what method you've used in the past. Continue to use whichever method you've been using. You can't arbitrarily switch back and forth from one method to another from year to year. If you think you have reason to switch, check with a tax professional for the proper procedures for making a change in Accounting Method. It can be done, but you better get some help to do it right.

If this is your first year in business, you can choose either method. If you have many outstanding invoices as of December 31, you'll pay less tax for 2015 if you use the Cash Method. You will have to report the income in 2016 when those invoices get paid, so over the two years you end up paying the same amount of tax either way.

Chapter 5. How to Deduct Advertising Expense on Schedule C, Line 8

If you are serious about growing your Sole Proprietorship, you likely incur advertising expenses every year. The purpose of this chapter is to make sure you are not missing any of the typical advertising expenses common to Sole Proprietors.

The big picture. Let's use a two-fold categorization of advertising expenses: Offline Advertising and Online Advertising.

Offline Advertising Expenses.

Print Advertisting Media. This includes space ads in newspapers, magazines and newsletters.

Coupon Decks. This includes Val-Pak and other similar cooperative advertising efforts.

Radio and Television Advertising. This is frequently the most expensive type of advertising, so don't forget to deduct any commercials you pay for, as well as any costs associated with the production of those commercials.

Copywriting. Did you hire a professional copywriter?

Other Printed Promotional Materials such as Sale Letters, Brochures and Catalogues. The costs to create, produce and distribute these items are all deductible.

Billboards. Got any of those around town?

Online Advertising Expenses.

Website expenses. If you use your website as a promotional tool, there are many expenses involved here, such as website hosting services and your internet service provider.

Search Engine Optimization. Do you spend money to make sure your website is properly optimized for search engine results?

Pay-Per-Click Advertising. Yahoo and Google are the two most popular service providers in this arena.

Ezine Ads. Do you place space ads in online newsletters?

Banner Ads. Do you spend money to hang your shingle on other websites in cyberspace?

Affiliate Program. Do you spend any money to promote and maintain an affiliate program? The biggest expense here is likely the commissions you are paying your affiliates to sell your products for you.

Chapter 6. How to Deduct Actual Vehicle Expenses on Schedule C, Line 9

As a Sole Proprietor, are you looking for an easy way to increase expenses and reduce your tax bill? Look no further than the vehicle you drive every day. The tax code says you can deduct the cost of purchasing and maintaining your car, to the extent you use that car for business. The purpose of this chapter is to help you claim this deduction to the fullest extent allowed by law.

There are two legal ways to deduct car-related expenses: the Mileage Method and the Actual Expense Method. We will focus on the Actual Expense Method in this chapter and the Mileage Method in the next chapter.

Keep in mind, however, that if you use your vehicle less than 100% for business, the Actual Expense Method requires that you keep track of the mileage as well as all the receipts for actual expenses. Most Sole Proprietors use the same vehicle for both personal and business use. So if you are using the Actual Expense Method, after you add up all those expenses, you have to know the "Business Use Percentage" to arrive at the deductible portion of your actual expenses. You calculate the Business Use Percentage by dividing business miles by total miles. Example: you have 10,000 total miles and 8,000 business miles, resulting in a Business Use Percentage of 80%. If you have $5,000 of actual expenses, you don't get to deduct the entire $5,000. Instead, your deduction would be $5,000 x 80% = $4,000.

SCHEDULE C TAX DEDUCTIONS REVEALED

Since the only way that you can determine the Business Use Percentage is to track total miles and business miles, you must keep a mileage log in which you record your business miles. This log doesn't have to be fancy. Just keep a notebook in your car and every time you drive the car for business, record the date, purpose of the trip, and the number of miles driven. To calculate total miles for the year, simply subtract the December 31 odometer reading from the January 1 odometer reading.

Now comes the fun part: what types of vehicle expenses are deductible? Here's a good list to help you think like an accountant:

Gasoline
Oil
Repair work (both parts and labor)
Routine maintenance (such as oil changes and tune-ups, again both parts and labor)
Insurance
License and registration fees
Auto club dues
Car loan interest
Lease expense
State and local taxes
Depreciation and/or Section 179 expense

Parking and tolls. Good news: these expenses 100% deductible when incurred during business use of the vehicle.

Chapter 7. How to Deduct Vehicle Mileage Expense on Schedule C, Line 9

For the typical Sole Proprietor, taking a deduction for business use of your vehicle is one of the best ways to legitimately reduce your taxable income and pay less tax. This chapter will walk you through the process of reporting vehicle mileage on Schedule C, Line 9.

The IRS has authorized two methods of reporting vehicle-related expenses. The previous chapter dealt with Method #1 -- the "Actual Expense Method," in which you keep track of all vehicle expenses such as gasoline, oil, maintenance, repairs, car washes, insurance, depreciation and so on. Method #2 is known as the "Mileage Method" will be the focus of this chapter.

Instead of tracking and reporting actual expenses, the Mileage Method only requires you to track mileage. You simply keep a log of your vehicle business use and at the end of the year you add up all those miles and multiply that mileage number by a rate established by the IRS. In 2015 that mileage rate is 57.5 cents per mile. If you drove your car 10,000 miles for business purposes, you simply multiply 10,000 miles by .575 to arrive at your vehicle deduction of $5,750. Then you report that $5,750 deduction on Schedule C, Line 9.

There are two main advantages to the Mileage Method:

SCHEDULE C TAX DEDUCTIONS REVEALED

1. It is generally easier and less time consuming than tracking actual expenses. Think about it. With the Actual Expense method, you have to keep track of every receipt for every expense associated with your vehicle: every gas purchase, every repair or routine maintenance work such as oil changes and tune-ups, every car wash. With the Mileage Method, all you have to do is keep track of the mileage, which is easily done with a simple mileage log that you keep in your glove compartment. Every time you use the car for business, you record the date, the business purpose of the trip, and the mileage amount.

2. The Mileage Method may result in a larger deduction than the Actual Expense Method. Of course, the only way to know this for sure is to keep track of actual expenses as well as mileage. Then, at the end of the year, run the numbers both ways and see which method gives you the higher deduction. But for many folks, the difference is so insignificant that the time-saving benefit of the Mileage Method is well worth it.

Chapter 8. How to Deduct Commissions and Fees on Schedule C, Line 10

The Sole Proprietor has a multitude of legitimate deductible business expenses. Line 10 of Schedule C describes an expense that is often overlooked (and for good reason). When you go to the IRS instructions for Schedule C, there is literally no description at all for commission and fees. No wonder folks aren't sure what to put here. So let's take a closer look to make sure you aren't missing out on this deduction.

Let's discuss commissions first. And let's start by remembering that any commissions you pay to employees would not be reported on Line 10. Any employee compensation such as wages, salaries, bonuses and commissions should be reported on Line 26. Unfortunately, Line 26 is labeled "Wages", but this is misleading because "Wages" means any type of employee compensation. So if you are going to report commissions on Line 10, it must be commission paid to non-employees, such as an independent contractor.

Now let's discuss fees. Again, the IRS has not been very clear when it comes to the reporting of fees expense on Schedule C. Could there be a word more vague than "fees"? In addition, there are other line items that refer to expenses that could be considered a fee, such as Line 17, Legal and professional services (which would include attorney fees, accountant fees, consulting fees, and the like). And then there's Line 27, Other expenses, which is the perfect place to report any miscellaneous expenses not reported anywhere else on Schedule C, such as internet service provider fees, website hosting fees, and so on.

So if you have already put all your "fees" elsewhere on Schedule C, and are hard pressed to find any fees to report on Line 10, don't be concerned. As long as you have reported those fees somewhere on Schedule C, you are in good shape. It doesn't really matter to the IRS whether you put internet service provider fees on Line 27 or Line 10. The important thing is whether any fees you deduct are bona fide business expenses. The specific line you use to report those fees is not that important.

Chapter 9. How to Deduct Contract Labor on Schedule C, Line 11

Sole Proprietors are entitled to deduct all fees paid to independent contractors as a legitimate business expense. This expense is reported on Line 11 of Schedule C and is described there as "Contract Labor." The purpose of this chapter is to help you better understand this expense and how to deduct it without worry.

Let's start with a definition. The term "contract labor" is somewhat confusing because when we use the word "labor" we often think of employee compensation such as wages and salaries. Well, Line 11 of Schedule C is definitely NOT referring to employee compensation. Rather it is referring to non-employee compensation to people such as independent contractors, consultants, and the like. These are other businesses that are providing a service to your business. These other businesses could be self-employed Sole Proprietors or other business entities such as a Corporation, Partnership or a Limited Liability Company (LLC).

In light of the above, a more succinct definition of contract labor is this: expenses paid for services rendered by non-employees.

While the word "labor" tends to confuse the issue, the word "contract" certainly helps clarify it. There are three things you can do to ensure the validity of this deduction:

1) Put the terms of your agreement with any independent contract in writing. In other words, if you are hiring an

independent contractor, shouldn't there be a contract? It doesn't have to be long or elaborate, nor does it have to be drafted by an attorney. But doesn't it make good business sense to put it in writing?

2) If you pay an independent contractor $600 or more during a calendar year and that independent contractor is a Sole Proprietor, you must issue a Form 1099-MISC to the contractor and file a copy of both Form 1099-MISC and 1096 with the IRS. Generally speaking, Sole Proprietorships are the main recipients of a Form 1099-MISC. Payments to corporations, partnerships and LLC's are typically excluded from this requirement (although there are some exceptions), as well as payments for products and payments to employees (who receive Form W-2 instead).

3) If you are paying an independent contractor, this contractor should be giving you an invoice for the services performed. If he/she is truly in business for himself and not an employee, isn't this just common sense?

NOTE: I'm going to skip Schedule C, Line 12, Depletion. Hardly anybody takes that deduction, so chances are you don't get to take it either.

THE PLAIN ENGLISH GUIDE TO 101 SELF-EMPLOYED TAX BREAKS

CHAPTER 10. HOW TO DEDUCT BUSINESS EQUIPMENT ON SCHEDULE C, LINE 13

If you are a Sole Proprietor who purchased business equipment, and you'd like to deduct that purchase on your income tax return without breaking into a sweat, this chapter is for you. I'm going to show you how to properly fill out Form 4562 without getting bogged down in those complex depreciation calculations, and you'll get to deduct the full price of your equipment in the year you bought it.

This chapter is all about taking a deduction for business equipment on Schedule D, Line 13 – "Depreciation and Section 179 expense deduction." Actually, I'm only going to explain how to take the Section 179 deduction. Depreciation is another animal, and we're not going to deal with that in this book. It's way too complicated for a book like this. If you don't meet the four conditions described below to take the Section 179 deduction, and you've purchased personal property and/or real property that needs to be depreciated, you should get some help from a tax professional who knows about depreciation.

There are four conditions that must be met in order for this chapter to apply to your situation.

1) You must have purchased less than $500,000 worth of business equipment during the year.

2) This equipment must be personal property (such as computers, printers, other office machinery like a phone or fax machine, office furniture, or any other

type of business machinery) not real estate (such as an office building, storefront property or warehouse).

3) Before considering the cost of your equipment, you have a profit in your business, and that profit amount is greater than the total purchase price of equipment bought during the year.

4) These items are only used for business purposes. You didn't buy anything that is used partly for business use and partly for personal use.

Now, you may be thinking, "Wow. Those are a lot of hoops to jump through." But not really. This is really a very common situation. You have a business. And you bought business equipment that is used exclusively in the business. And you are a small business owner, so we're not talking about spending hundreds of thousands of dollars, even thousands of dollars. For example, you may have bought a new computer for $500 and a new printer for $200. And that's it. That's a very simply situation and reporting those purchases on your income tax return should be a simple procedure. And guess what: it is!

Here's all you have to do in the above scenario. Go to Form 4562 and put $700 on Line 2, which is labeled "Total cost of section 179 property placed in service." Then go to Line 6 and put a brief description of these two items in column (a). You'd put "Computer" on the first line and "Printer" on the second line. Then go to Line 6, column (b) and put the purchase price (or "Cost"); so you'd put $500 on the first line and $200 on the second line. Then go to Line 6, column (c) and put the same amounts as column (b). Column (c) is labeled "Elected cost".

Then go to Line 8 and put the total cost of both items, which is $700. Go to Line 9 and again put $700. Then go to Line 12 and again put $700. Then all the way down to Line 22 and again put $700. And that's it. You are done with Form 4562.

Notice that we skipped several lines in Part I, and we also skipped all the lines in Part II and Part III. Don't worry about them. Since you met the four conditions listed above, you don't have to put anything on those lines.

Now there is one more thing you must do. Take the amount from Line 22 ($700) and transfer it to Schedule C, Line 13, which is where you actually get to take the deduction for the computer and printer.

One more tip: what if you bought more than two items of business equipment? Simply list all the items on a separate schedule, showing the description, cost and elected cost, exactly as described above. Take the total from this schedule and put that on Line 6, columns (b) and (c), and put the words "See attached schedule" on Line 6, column (a).

To get the latest on the Section 179 deduction, visit http://www.section179.org/. This is an excellent website with accurate and timely information related to the Section 179 deduction.

SCHEDULE C TAX DEDUCTIONS REVEALED

IMPORTANT NEWS FLASH

In late 2015, the IRS issued new rules that effectively eliminate the requirement for many Schedule C filers from reporting their business equipment purchases on Form 4562. This is wonderful news!

Here's how it works. If the purchase price of any business equipment is less than $2,500, the item does not have to be reported on Form 4562. Instead, assuming the item is used 100% for business, you can simply report 100% of the purchase price on Line 22, Supplies.

The end result is identical to taking the Section 179 deduction explained earlier. But this is even better: by reporting the purchase on Line 22, you avoid the hassle of filing Form 4562.

Believe it or not, every now and then, the IRS does something that makes our tax system a little easier to deal with. This is one such occasion.

Chapter 11. How to Deduct Employee Benefits On Schedule C, Line 14

If you are a Sole Proprietor with employees, there are numerous employee benefits that you can deduct on Schedule C, Line 14. Are you aware of what those are? If not, read on and get the scoop on this type of deductible small business expense.

First, let's discuss what should not be deducted on Line 14. Note that the Schedule C description for Line 14 reads as follows: "Employee benefit programs (other than line 19)." So we go to Line 19 and read "Pension and profit-sharing plans." In other words, do not include pension plan expenses or other employer-provided retirement plan expenses on Line 14.

Now on to the good news: what kinds of expenses can you deduct on Line 14? Here's an overview of the most common types of employee benefit plans:

Accident and Health Insurance Plans.

Do you provide a health insurance plan for your employees? The premiums you pay are a deductible business expense for you and a tax-free benefit to your employees. Some employers pay 100% of the premium on behalf of their employees. Others share the expense, with the employer paying part and the employee paying part. If you are sharing the expense, be sure to only deduct your part of the premium payment.

Also, be careful not to deduct any health insurance premium you pay for yourself on Line 14. Self-employed individuals are not considered an employee of the Sole Proprietorship, so you are not allowed to deduct your own health insurance premiums on Schedule C. You may still qualify for a health insurance deduction, but you must take the deduction on Form 1040, Line 29. Check the rules on that, however, as there are specific criteria for qualifying.

One more comment here: If your spouse happens to be an employee of your business, you can put her on the health insurance policy as the primary insured, and you would be covered as one of her dependent family members. End result: you do get to deduct your own health insurance premium on Schedule C. There are at least two tax advantages to this approach: 1) You don't have to qualify for the Form 1040, Line 29 deduction, which is disallowed if you have a loss on Schedule C; and 2) Taking a deduction on Schedule C rather than Form 1040 reduces not only your federal income tax, but also your Self-Employment Tax, resulting in an approximate 15% additional tax savings.

Group Term Life Insurance Plans.

Again, you only get to take this deduction for your employees, not for yourself. Sorry!

Dependent Care Assistance Programs.

This is an employer sponsored program that provides reimbursements for up to $2,500 annually ($5,000 for married couples), to employees who pay for dependent care if certain conditions are met. Employees are allowed to deduct dependent care expenses from their paycheck on a pre-tax basis. Employees who are enrolled in this type of program are not eligible to claim the Child and Dependent Care Credit on their tax return. For more information, see IRS Publication 15-B, Employer's Tax Guide to Fringe Benefits, available at www.IRS.gov/publications/p15b/ar02.html

Chapter 12. How to Deduct Insurance on Schedule C, Line 15

There are many bona fide business expenses that are often overlooked by Sole Proprietors. One of them is insurance. Here's what you need to know to properly deduct insurance expense on your Schedule C.

Insurance that's deductible on Schedule C includes:

1. Business liability/malpractice insurance and property casualty insurance.

Insurance that covers your business or business property is deductible. Most small businesses have some type of coverage to protect you, your employees and your property in the event of a lawsuit or some type of property damage caused by theft, fire, flood or other natural disaster like a bad storm or an electrical failure. So be sure to write off those kinds of insurance premiums on Line 15.

2. Health insurance for employees. It probably doesn't matter much whether you deduct this on Line 15 (insurance) or Line 14 (Employee benefit programs), but I prefer to think of it as an employee benefit and so recommend you put it on Line 14.

3. Workers' compensation insurance. Report this on Line 15.

4. Vehicle insurance. If you are using the Actual Expense Method, your vehicle insurance is deductible to the extent the vehicle is used for business (as determined by the business use mileage percentage). You can report the deductible portion of insurance on either Line 15 (insurance) or Line 9

(car and truck expenses). If you are using the Mileage Rate Method to deduct vehicle expense, then the insurance on your vehicle is not deductible.

There are two kinds of insurance that are deductible, just not on Schedule C.

1. Homeowner's insurance or renter's insurance for those who are taking the Home Office deduction. If you calculate for the Business Use of Home deduction on Form 8829, you can deduct a portion of your homeowner's/renter's insurance. You include the insurance premium on Form 8829 and then the business use portion is calculated on that form and transferred to Schedule C, Line 30. If you use the "simplified method" to calculate the home office deduction, then you do not deduct the actual cost of homeowner's insurance or renter's insurance.

2. Health insurance for the owner. This is never deductible on Schedule C. Instead, report it on Form 1040, Line 29, "Self-employed health insurance deduction." Are you wondering, "Why isn't health insurance for the owner treated the same as health insurance for employees?" Answer: Because the owner of a Sole Proprietorship is never considered to be an employee of the business.

How about life insurance? As explained in the previous chapter, life insurance for your employees is reported on Line 14, Employee benefit programs. Life insurance on the owner is a non-deductible personal expense. Sorry!

Chapter 13. How to Deduct Interest on Schedule C, Line 16

Interest expense is a deductible expense for Sole Proprietors on Schedule C, Line 16. The purpose of this chapter is to make sure you take advantage of the many types of interest expense you are likely to incur in your small business.

Line 16 of Schedule C offers two main categories of interest expense: Mortgage interest (Line 16a) and Other (Line 16b). Let's take a closer look at each of these categories.

Mortgage Interest.

If you purchase real estate for use in your business, such as a commercial office building or a storefront property, and take out a mortgage on that property, the interest expense on that loan is 100% deductible. Be sure to deduct this interest here (on Schedule C) rather than as a personal itemized deduction (on Schedule A). The reason: interest deducted on Schedule C is worth more in tax savings than interest deducted on Schedule A, because any Schedule C expense will reduce both income tax and self-employment tax; any Schedule A deduction will reduce only income tax.

Another word of caution: If you are taking the Home Office deduction, be sure to deduct the business portion of your residential mortgage interest on Form 8829 rather than here on Schedule C. The business portion of that interest will flow from Form 8829 to your Schedule C, Line 30.

Other Interest.

There are several types of valid non-mortgage business interest. Two of the most common are:

1. Auto loan interest, to the extent the vehicle was used for business. So, if your vehicle is used 100% for business, than 100% of the auto loan interest is deductible. Most Sole Proprietors drive the same car for both business and personal use, so you will have to apply the business use percentage (business miles divided by total miles) to the auto loan interest to determine the deductible amount. Helpful tip: you get to deduct auto loan interest regardless of whether you use the Actual Expense Method or the Mileage Rate Method.

2. Credit card interest, again, to the extent that the items purchased with that credit card are used for your business. If you have a credit card that is used exclusively for business items, then any interest or finance charges are fully deductible. But if you are using that credit card for both personal and business items, you'll have to do an allocation based on the purchase price of the various items charged to that account. Helpful tip: pick one credit card that you use exclusively for business purchases and you can avoid dealing with the allocation calculation.

Chapter 14. How to Deduct Legal & Professional Services on Schedule C, Line 17

Sole Proprietors are entitled to deduct the cost of services provided by lawyers, accountants and other professionals on Schedule C, Line 17. Let's take a closer look at this often overlooked deduction.

First, an obvious comment: like any legitimate business expense, legal and professional services are only deductible if they were performed for your business. Personal professional service fees are not deductible on Schedule C.

Now let's brainstorm some examples of valid professional services that you are likely to incur as an ordinary and necessary business expense:

Legal services: Hiring an attorney to draft contracts and other business-related documents is probably the most common example of a deductible legal expense. Any legal fees you incur in the unfortunate event of a business-related lawsuit are also deductible. Another common legal fee these days is the cost for membership in a pre-paid legal services plan.

Accounting services: Any fees you pay for bookkeeping, financial statement preparation, payroll processing, payroll tax return preparation, income tax return preparation, sales tax return preparation, tax consulting, etc. are all deductible.

Here's a common situation that needs clarification: Since you are a Sole Proprietor, is it valid to deduct the cost of personal income tax return preparation, since the fee would include the preparation of Schedule C and other business-related forms such as Schedule SE, Form 4562, and Form 8829? Technically, your accountant is also charging you for preparation of non-business forms such as Form 1040, Schedule A and Schedule B, so you will want to ask your accountant to provide a breakdown of his fees. It's not necessary for him to itemize the cost of every individual form, but he does need to allocate his fee into at least two parts: personal forms and business forms, as mentioned above.

Consulting services: The cost of hiring a consultant to help you establish, grow or improve your business is certainly a valid business expense, and increasingly common these days. Virtually every aspect of business has a corresponding consulting profession. Here is partial list of the types of consultants you may need to hire eventually, if you haven't already: sales and marketing, employee relations, customer service, financial management, entity and tax planning.

Chapter 15. How to Deduct Office Expenses on Schedule C, Line 18

One of the most common business deductions for the Sole Proprietor is office expense. While this expense is not usually overlooked by the typical small business owner, there are a few potential pitfalls you should be aware of.

The kinds of items typically included in office expense are obvious: postage, copy paper, stationary, file folders, staplers and staples, pens/pencils/markers, etc. Virtually every little item on your desk is a deduction.

What is not so obvious are the items that often end up on Line 18 that should be deducted elsewhere. Here are a couple of these to watch out for:

Home Office Expense. If you qualify for the home office deduction, aka the "Business Use of Home" deduction, by all means take it! But it does not belong on Schedule C, Line 18. Instead, you must complete Form 8829, Expenses for Business Use of Your Home. The total expense from Form 8829 is then transferred to Schedule C, Line 30.

Office Equipment and other depreciable personal property. Things like computers, monitors, printers, telephones, fax machines, desks, file cabinets, bookcases and so forth – these are commonly found in an office, so shouldn't they be reported in the "Office expense" line of Schedule C? No. These items are known as "fixed assets" or "depreciable property" and they must first be reported on Form 4562. Many Sole Proprietors quality for a nifty write-off known as the Section

179 deduction, which entitles you to fully deduct the cost of these items in the year of purchase; but to qualify for the Section 179 deduction, you must first list these things on Form 4562 and then transfer the Section 179 deduction amount from Form 4562 to Schedule C, Line 13, "Deprecation and Section 179 expense deduction." This whole area of depreciation and fixed assets is not for the financially faint of heart, so if you're not well-versed on this topic, please consult with a tax professional.

Chapter 16. How to Deduct Retirement Plan Expense on Schedule C, Line 19

Do you provide a tax-deductible retirement plan to the employees of your Sole Proprietorship? If so, this chapter is to explain the ins and outs of how to properly deduct any expenses related to such plans on your Schedule C.

If you look at Schedule C, Line 19, you'll notice it says "Pension and profit-sharing plans." For many Sole Proprietors, does such language cause your head to spin while reaching for the Tylenol? Yes, such wording can seem archaic to us. Does anyone still have a pension plan? The answer to that question is Yes, but there are several other types of retirement plans that are more common these days, and any expenses you incur to setup, maintain and contribute to an employer-sponsored employee retirement plan are usually deductible.

Here are the more common types of retirement plans you should consider offering to your employees:

1. Simplified Employee Pension Plan, also known as a SEP.

2. Savings Incentive Match Plan for Employees, better known as a SIMPLE Plan.

3. Keogh Plan.

4. 401(k) Plan.

Each of these plans has different features and benefits for both your employees and yourself, so you would do well to research each one thoroughly before deciding which one is best for you, your business and your employees.

Some of these plans allow you to make tax-deductible contributions on behalf of your employees. Some of these plans also allow your employees to make voluntary pre-tax contributions to the plan from their compensation. And some of these plans have a matching provision in which you make a contribution to the plan only if the employee makes a contribution. So there is quite a variety of options here.

For more information on the different retirement plans available to Sole Proprietors, check out IRS Publication 560, Retirement Plans for Small Business, available for free at the IRS website, or consult with your tax or investment professional.

Two other important warnings related to small business retirement plans:

1. Contributions on behalf of yourself are generally not reported on Schedule C. They are instead deducted on Form 1040, Line 28, "Self-employed SEP, SIMPLE, and qualified plans."

2. Some retirement plans require you to file an information return -- Form 5500 or Form 5500-EZ. Be sure to find out whether your plan has such a requirement.

Chapter 17. How to Deduct Rent & Lease Expense on Schedule C, Line 20

There are literally dozens if not hundreds of deductible expenses available to the typical Sole Proprietor. Some of these are more obvious than others, such as rent and lease expense. Let's take a closer look to make sure you're not missing out on this deduction.

Schedule C, Line 20 provides two sub-categories for rent/lease expense:

Line 20a – Vehicles, machinery and equipment.

Let's start with "machinery and equipment." Businesses often lease office equipment like computers, copy machines and the like. If the leased equipment is being used 100% for business, then the lease expense is 100% deductible. As far as vehicles are concerned, it is more likely that you are not using the vehicle 100% for business, as most Sole Proprietors drive the same car for both business and personal use. If that's the case, you'll have to do an allocation of the lease expense based on the business use percentage, which is calculated by dividing business miles by total miles. Then apply that business use percentage to the lease expense to determine the deductible portion of the lease expense.

Keep in mind, too, that vehicle lease expense is only deductible if you are using the Actual Expense Method. If you are using the Mileage Rate Method, then the lease expense is not deductible at all. The Mileage Method uses the IRS-authorized standard mileage rate to determine your vehicle expense, in lieu of actual expenses such as lease, gasoline, maintenance, repairs, insurance, etc.

Line 20b – Other business property. This is where you report the most common type of rent or lease expense: the cost of renting your office, store, warehouse, or other commercial building. For many small business owners, this is one of your largest expenses, if not the largest. So don't forget to deduct it!

Chapter 18. How to Deduct Repairs and Maintenance Expense on Schedule C, Line 21

At first glance, deducting repairs and maintenance expense seems like a no-brainer for the average Sole Proprietor. But all is not what it may appear to be, and such is the case with this expense. It's critical that you understand some important rules that govern the deductibility of both repairs and maintenance expense.

What is fully deductible must be a true repair or maintenance expense. You can deduct the cost of parts and labor in order to repair or maintain your business assets, provided that this expense does not increase the value of the asset or prolong the useful life of the asset. This is one of the most important yet misunderstood tax rules on the books. The tax code makes a clear distinction between a repair/maintenance expense and an improvement. A repair/maintenance expense is fully deductible in the year the expense is incurred.

What is not fully deductible is what must be depreciated. An improvement (which is defined above as the cost to increase the value or prolong the life of an asset) is not fully deductible in the year the expense in incurred. Instead, an improvement to non-residential commercial real estate (i.e. business property such as an office building, storefront, warehouse) must be depreciated over a period of 39 years.

Do you see the huge difference here between a repair/maintenance expense and a depreciable improvement? If you spend $5,000 to spruce up your office or storefront, it is critical that you properly determine whether this cost is 100% deductible in the year the work was done, or whether the cost must be depreciated on 39 years, which would mean you only get to deduct $128 each year for many years to come! Certainly this is a tricky area, and if you are not sure how to apply this rule regarding the difference between a repair and an improvement, be sure to consult a competent tax professional.

Here are three more criteria to determine whether work done is a repair or an improvement: 1) To be a repair, the work must not adapt the asset to a different use; 2) To be a repair, the work must not restore the asset, as this would be deemed an attempt to extend the life of the asset; and 3) Replacing an asset is not a repair.

Chapter 19. How to Deduct Supplies on Schedule C, Line 22

One of the most common deductible expenses for Sole Proprietors is supplies. You've got office supplies, cleaning supplies, and who knows how many other types of supplies related to the typical small business. The challenge isn't so much knowing that supplies are a valid deduction, but rather knowing where on Schedule C to report your supplies. That is the purpose of this article.

There are at least four lines on Schedule C where it is appropriate to deduct supplies expense:

Line 18. Office expense. Obviously, office supplies should go here. By office supplies we're referring to all the little things used in a business office: from pens and paper to staples and staplers, and everything in between.

Line 21. Repairs and maintenance. Any parts used to repair or maintain business equipment can be reported here.

Line 38. Materials and supplies. This is part of Part III of Schedule C, Cost of Goods Sold, where retailers and manufacturers report the expenses related to the sale of products. Any supplies used in the production of goods for resale should be reported here.

Line 22. Supplies. Here's where you can put anything else that falls under the category of supplies but not shown on Lines 18, 21 or 38. There are likely certain supplies that are unique to your particular business or industry. I'm an accountant and so I prepare hundreds of tax returns every year and there are certain supplies related to tax return preparation I need that you may not need, simply because you are not an accountant. For example, every year I purchase a nifty item called the "Tax Organizer & Problem Minimizer." It's a 20-page booklet that I give out to my clients to help them get organized and make sure they've collected all the information needed to properly prepare their income tax returns. That is a supply unique to the tax return preparation business. If you are a barber, you will have supplies unique to your business, such as towels and scissors and shaving cream. I think you get the idea.

Chapter 20. How to Deduct Taxes on Schedule C, Line 23

This chapter explains the ins and outs of Schedule C, Line 23. It is labeled "Taxes and licenses."

"Licenses" is self-explanatory. The fee you pay to obtain a license required for your business is deductible.

Now let's focus on "taxes." Sole Proprietors are entitled to deduct certain types of taxes they incur in their business, so it's important that you know what types of taxes are deductible and what types are not deductible.

Non-deductible Taxes.

First, the bad news. There are several types of taxes that you do not get to deduct on Schedule C. The most obvious is federal income tax. So sorry to disappoint you, but that's just the way it is. In fact, you don't get to deduct federal income tax anywhere on your federal personal income tax return.

How about state income tax? Well, that is not deductible on Schedule C, but it is deductible on Schedule A, Itemized Deductions, Line 5. So be sure to report it there.

Next comes what is probably the most hated tax of every Sole Proprietor, the dreaded Self-Employment (SE) Tax, which is calculated on Schedule SE and reported on Form 1040, Line 57. Well, I've got good news and bad news on this. The bad news is that is it not fully deductible. The good news is that it is partially deductible. One-half of your SE tax is deductible on

Form 1040, Line 27. In effect, this 50% deduction reduces your actual SE tax rate to less than 15.3%.

Deductible Taxes.

OK, how about some good news? There are several taxes that are fully deductible on Schedule C, Line 23. Here they are.

State and/or local property taxes on business assets. This would include any real estate taxes you pay on land or other buildings used in your business. Also included in this would be personal property taxes on business assets, including any personal property tax on your vehicle (to the extent the vehicle was used for business).

State and/or local sales tax. If you report the sales tax collected from customers in your sales total on Line 1, be sure to also report it here as an expense. If you don't report the sales tax as part of sales, then you don't get to report it as an expense.

Payroll taxes. If you have employees and report wages on Schedule C, Line 26, there are four main payroll taxes you also get to deduct: the employer's share of social security tax, the employer's share of Medicare tax, federal unemployment tax, and state unemployment tax.

Chapter 21. How to Deduct Travel Expenses on Schedule C, Line 24a

Travel expenses are another of those "obvious" expenses that most Sole Proprietors incur. It is also one of the most abused small business expenses, so it's important that you understand the basic rules so as not to run afoul of the IRS in the event of an audit. And Line 24a (along with 24b, Meals) is one of the most frequently audited lines on Schedule C. So the purpose of this chapter is to explain the rules on travel expenses so that you know what you can and cannot deduct. If you follow these rules carefully and are ever audited, you'll have nothing to worry about.

The first "ground rule" is the obvious one: the travel expenses must be related to an overnight trip of a business purpose. You can only deduct travel expenses for yourself and your employees. If your spouse or children happen to travel with you, their travel expenses are not deductible, unless your spouse or child is an employee of your business and there is a bona fide business purpose for their presence on the trip.

The two most common types of deductible travel expenses are transportation and lodging. Let's take a close look at both of them.

Transportation is the cost of getting to and from your destination. It can include the cost of traveling by plane, train or bus, or any other form or public transportation. If you drive your own car, you would deduct the transportation expense based on whether you are using the Mileage Method or the Actual Expense Method for your vehicle.

Lodging is the cost of staying in a hotel or motel. What happens if your spouse travels with you and your spouse is not your employee? How do you determine the deduction for the hotel room? If the cost of the room is the same regardless of the number of people staying in the room, then you get to deduct the actual cost of the room. But if the cost of two people is more than the cost of one person, your deduction is the one-person room rate, not the two-person room rate.

What about the cost of meals? You do get to deduct meals while on an overnight business trip, but not on Line 24a. Meals expenses, for either overnight business trips or for local business meals, are deductible on Line 24b.

With regard to both lodging and meals, you can deduct the actual cost of the expense (for meals, that means actual cost times 50%) or you can take a deduction based on the Per Diem Method, regardless of the actual expense amount. A per diem is a standard IRS-approved amount determined by the location of the trip. For details on per diem rates and how they work, visit http://www.gsa.gov/portal/content/104877

There are other deductible travel expenses besides transportation and lodging, such as:

--local transportation during your stay, i.e. taxi, commuter bus and airport limousine;

--baggage and shipping expenses related to your travel

--dry cleaning and laundry expenses related to your travel

--telephone calls during the trip

--tips incurred for any of the other items mentioned above

--other ordinary and necessary expenses related to the travel.

See IRS Publication 463 for more information on business travel deductions.

Chapter 22. How to Deduct Meals Expenses on Schedule C, Line 24b

One of the most frequently audited lines on the Sole Proprietor's federal income tax return is Schedule C, Line 24b – meals. And the reason is probably no surprise – it's an area that is often exaggerated and prone to abuse. So you've got to watch your "P's and Q's" here. Knowing the basics for deducting meals will give you a head start in winning this battle, so if you pay attention to the rules explained in this chapter, you'll have no trouble should the IRS ever come calling for documentation.

There are two types of meals that are deductible:

1. Meals you eat during overnight business travel (when you are in "business travel status"). These meals are deductible whether you eat alone or with other people. And these meals are deductible whether or not you have a business relationship with the other people you happen to eat with. In other words, all meals while traveling away from home overnight are deductible. If you do eat with other people and pay for the meals of those other people, you can only deduct the cost of their meals if you have a business relationship with those people, and you engage in a substantive business discussion before, during or after the meal.

2. Meals you eat when you are not in business travel status, provided you eat with people with whom you have a business relationship, and provided you engage in a substantive business discussion in conjunction with (i.e. before, during or after) the meal.

Other important rules governing the meals deduction include:

1. Business meals are deductible only if they are not lavish or extravagant.

2. Business meals are deductible only if you or one of your employees is physically present at the meal.

3. You only get to deduct 50% of the cost of the meal. So, on Schedule C, Line 24b, be careful not to report the total cost of your meals. You must multiply that total cost by 50% and report that amount on Line 24b.

Chapter 23. How to Deduct Utilities on Schedule C, Line 25

If you are a Sole Proprietor and are looking for all the deductions the tax law allows you to take, make sure you properly deduct utilities on Schedule C. This chapter will give you the details on the do's and don'ts of utility expense deductions.

What you can deduct.

Let's start with the good news. If you have a business location that is separate from your personal residence, such as an office, a store, a warehouse, or other commercial building (regardless of whether you own or rent this structure), you are entitled to fully deduct all utilities expenses. This would include the obvious: electricity, gas, water, sewer service, waste disposal and telephone service. All these expenses should be reported on Schedule C, Line 25.

What you cannot deduct.

Now comes the bad news. Sole Proprietors who work out of their home often assume they can take a deduction for their home phone line. This is especially true of those who qualify for the home office deduction. I'm sorry to disappoint you, but if you only have one line coming into your home, you can never deduct the base rate for the first line into your residence, regardless of how much you use that line for business purposes.

Here's what you can deduct related to the business use of your home phone:

SCHEDULE C TAX DEDUCTIONS REVEALED

1. The cost of any additional lines into your home that are used exclusively for business are deductible. For example, if you have a second line that is dedicated to business use, you can write off the expense associated with that line. Another example would be a second line that is used only as a business fax line.

2. Any long distance business charges are deductible, regardless of how many lines you have coming into your home. It is necessary to specifically identify those business calls on your monthly phone bills and add them up to determine the actual expense. You can even deduct business long distance calls on the first line.

Another important mistake you want to avoid is reporting your other home utility expenses (such as electricity, gas, water, etc.) on Schedule C, Line 25. If you qualify for the home office deduction, you are entitled to deduct the business use percentage of those home utilities, but you must report those expenses on Form 8829 first. The total of all your home office expenses is then transferred from Form 8829 to Schedule C, Line 30.

THE PLAIN ENGLISH GUIDE TO 101 SELF-EMPLOYED TAX BREAKS

Chapter 24. How to Deduct Wages on Schedule C, Line 26 (Part 1)

Do you own a Sole Proprietorship and have employees? If so, this chapter is for you. In addition to filing Schedule C, you'll have to file several payroll tax forms to report those employee wages and the related payroll taxes. Here's an overview of the entire compensation and payroll tax reporting process.

Schedule C.

To make sure that this chapter really does apply to you, go to your Schedule C and take a look at Line 26, Wages. This is where you report employee wages. If you have employees, you should report the total annual wage amount here. Please note that we are talking about employee wages reported on Form W-2, not independent contractor payments reported on Form 1099-MISC. There's a huge difference between those two kinds of compensation. Independent contractor payments are reported on Schedule C, but on Line 11, Contract labor.

If you are not sure whether you have employees only, independent contractors only, or both, be sure to consult with a tax professional to get the scoop on the rules to determine the difference between the two. This is a critical area that you do not want to report incorrectly. There are stiff penalties for paying an employee as an independent contractor. At the same time, you also don't want to pay a true independent contractor as an employee.

SCHEDULE C TAX DEDUCTIONS REVEALED

Form W-2.

All employees must receive a Form W-2 from you by January 31 of the following year. Example: all employees must receive a 2015 W-2 from you by January 31, 2016. This W-2 reports the employee's wages, federal, state and local income tax withholdings, Social Security and Medicare tax withholdings, and several miscellaneous payroll related items such as retirement plan contributions (if any).

Form W-3.

This form, along with a copy of Form W-2, must be sent to the Social Security Administration, usually by February 28 of the next year.

Form 941 - Employer's Quarterly Federal Tax Return.

As the name indicates, you must send this form to the IRS every quarter, by the end of the month following each calendar quarter. The dues dates are the end of April, July, October and January. This form reports total wages and federal withholding amounts (income tax, Social Security tax, Medicare tax) for each quarter.

Form 940. Employer's Annual Federal Unemployment (FUTA) Tax Return.

This form reports the employer's federal unemployment tax – which is a tax that every employer must pay. The tax is 0.6% of the first $7,000 of wages paid to each employee each calendar year. In recent years, some states have additional FUTA tax to pay and this amount varies from state to state.

State Unemployment Tax Return.

Most states have their own version of the FUTA tax mentioned above, and most states also require that this state unemployment tax be paid quarterly. So check with your particular state.

Chapter 25. How to Deduct Wages on Schedule C, Line 26 (Part 2)

This chapter could also be entitled, "What *Not* to Report As Wages on Schedule C, Line 26."

Let's continue our discussion of Schedule C, Line 26.

The purpose of this chapter is to help you further understand the purpose of Schedule C, Line 26, Wages. Whether or not you have employees, if you are a Sole Proprietor, it is critical that you properly deduct expenses related to compensation.

The purpose of Schedule C, Line 26 is to deduct employee compensation. The IRS has labeled this line "Wages," but employee compensation includes not only wages paid to hourly employees, but also salaries, commissions and bonuses paid to employees. The key here is this: whatever you pay your employees should be reported on this line.

With that in mind, let's discuss what should *not* be reported on Line 26. First, never report payments to yourself, the Sole Proprietor. The owner of a Sole Proprietorship is never considered to be an employee of the business. Any payments you make to yourself out of the business (sometimes called "draw") are considered a withdrawal of profit, not employee compensation.

The other big mistake is to report independent contractor payments on Line 26. If you have people that provide services to your business as independent contractors, report those payments on Schedule C, Line 11, Contract labor. And if these people are truly independent contractors, there should be a written contract between the two of you. Furthermore, if you pay a contractor $600 or more in a calendar year, you are required to issue him/her a Form 1099-MISC to report the total annual amount of non-employee compensation.

One final comment: if you report any employee compensation on Line 26, you must file several employee-related payroll tax returns on a regular basis. As discussed in the previous chapter, the most common federal payroll tax forms include Form 941 (quarterly), Form 940 (annually) and Forms W-2 and W-3 (annually). You may also be required to file payroll tax returns at the state level for state and local income tax withholdings, state unemployment tax and worker's compensation insurance, so be sure to check with your state for details on that.

Chapter 26. How to Deduct Miscellaneous Expenses on Schedule C, Line 27

For Sole Proprietors, Schedule C can be either your best friend or your biggest nightmare. There are parts of this two-page form that you will learn to love or hate. There are five parts to Schedule C, and the purpose of this chapter is to help you with Part V, Other Expenses – hopefully this will become one part of Schedule C that you come to enjoy preparing.

When you look at the "big picture" of Schedule C, you see right away that Part II is called "Expenses." This should bring a smile to the face of any savvy small business owner or self-employed person. But when you take a closer look at Part II, you see there are only about 20 expense categories. Starting with Line 8 (Advertising) and ending with Line 26 (Wages), they are listed in alphabetical order.

Perhaps you are wondering, "Only 20 expenses? You've got to be kidding me. Surely there are more legitimate expenses than that for the average Sole Proprietor." And you are correct. There are literally dozens, if not hundreds, of bona fide, legally deductible business expenses you are likely to incur in your small business. It just so happens that the IRS has not gone out of its way to tell you what those expenses are on Schedule C.

So what's a Sole Proprietor to do? That's where Part V of Schedule C comes into play. Actually, Part V is an expansion of Part II, Line 27, which comes right after the Wage expense category on Line 26. Line 27 reads "Other expenses." Ah, now we're getting somewhere. Then come the words, "from line 48 on page 2". Ah, now we're really getting somewhere. Line 48 on Page 2 of Schedule C is the summary line of Part V, Other Expenses.

So Part V is where you get to list all the "other" expenses for which the IRS didn't happen to include a separate line in Part II. Now, take note of the simple fact that even in Part V, there are only nine blank lines to record your other expenses. Even that may not be enough space for you to record all your other expenses. So where do you put them, if you happen to have more than nine? Simply use a separate sheet of paper and label it with your full name and social security number, along with the heading "Supporting Statement for Schedule C, Line 48." And then list all the valid expenses you have which do not happen to fall into one of the 20 expense categories found in Part II.

Chapter 27. How to Prepare Schedule C, Lines 33-42, Cost of Goods Sold (Part 1)

Are you a sole proprietor who sells a product? Then you need to know how to deduct expenses related to the sale of those products. The purpose of this chapter is to give you an overview of what is potentially your biggest tax deduction.

First, let's discuss an important concept related to this deduction known as "Cost of Goods Sold." Let's say in 2015 you start a business to sell widgets. You buy the widgets for $50 each and sell them for $100 each. Now it's tax time and you've got to figure out how to calculate the deduction for the cost of what you sold.

Here are only 2 possible scenarios. Scenario #1: You sell all the widgets that you bought. Let's assume you bought 100 widgets for $5,000 (100 widgets x $50) and sold all 100 widgets for $10,000 (100 widgets x $100). End result for tax purposes: you get to deduct the entire $5,000 that you spent to buy the widgets. $10,000 sales - $5,000 cost of goods sold = $5,000 Gross profit from sale of product.

Now let's move on to scenario #2: You sell some of the widgets, but not all of them. You bought 100 widgets for $5,000 (100 widgets x $50) but you only sold 50 widgets for $5,000 (50 widgets x $100). Do you still get to deduct the cost of all 100 widgets that you bought? No, you don't. You only get to deduct the cost of the widgets that were sold. If you didn't sell all the widgets, you don't get to deduct the cost of

THE PLAIN ENGLISH GUIDE TO 101 SELF-EMPLOYED TAX BREAKS

all the widgets. So here's how this scenario plays out: $5,000 sales - $2,500 cost of goods sold (50 widgets sold x $50) = $2,500 Gross profit from sale of product.

Still with me? It's critical that you understand this concept. If you don't sell all your product during the year, and still have some product sitting on the shelf at the end of year, don't make the mistake of deducting the cost of product you haven't yet sold.

Now let's discuss how all these numbers get reported on Schedule C. On page 1, notice that Line 4 is called "Cost of goods sold." So that's where you put the $5,000 from Scenario #1 or the $2,500 from Scenario #2. But that's just the end result of a slick calculation that you must do on page 2, Part III (Lines 33-42). This is the detailed Cost of Goods Sold section of Schedule C, and if you sell product, you must complete this section. Don't make the mistake of putting a number on page 1, Line 4 without filling out Part III, Lines 33-42. The Schedule C instructions do a good job of walking you through this section, line by line, so if you are preparing your own return, take the time to read those instructions for helpful tips.

If you hire an accountant to prepare your Schedule C, he/she should be well versed in the Cost of Goods Sold calculation, but you will still have to provide him/her with the annual totals for the following amounts:

1-Inventory at the beginning of the year.

2-Product purchased during the year.

3-Inventory at the end of the year.

SCHEDULE C TAX DEDUCTIONS REVEALED

If this is your first year in business, you won't have any inventory at the beginning of the year. And if you happen to sell all your product during the year, you won't have any inventory at the end of the year. But after you've been in business for a while, most product sellers have beginning and ending inventory, so you must keep track of that and be able to report than on your Schedule C every year. Once you know the three amounts listed above, it's easy to calculate cost of goods sold.

Chapter 28. How to Prepare Schedule C, Lines 33-42, Cost of Goods Sold (Part 2)

Let's continue our discussion of Lines 33-42 by taking a closer look.

If you are a Sole Proprietor whose business involves sale of a product, you must complete Part III of Schedule C, Cost of Goods Sold. The purpose of this chapter is to help you with this all-important task, because it is likely that Cost of Goods Sold is one of the largest expenses (if not the largest expense) in your business.

Part III of Schedule C begins on Page 2 of Schedule C, starting with Line 33 and ending with Line 42. Here's a "line-by-line" description of how to fill out each line.

Line 33. This is an information line, labeled "Method(s) used to value closing inventory". There are three choices: a) Cost; b) Lower of cost or market; c) Other. My advice is to use option "a" – Cost. The "closing inventory" (aka "ending inventory") is the value of any product you have remaining on hand at the end of the year. In other words, it represents what you bought that hasn't yet been sold. You will put the dollar amount of ending inventory on Line 41, so more about this in a moment.

Line 34. This is another information line. It's a "yes or no" question: Was there any change in determining quantities, costs, or valuations between opening and closing inventory? My advice: always answer this question with a "No." As long as you remain consistent from year to year and always value your ending inventory at your cost, you can answer this question "No" and move on.

Line 35. Inventory at beginning of year. If this is your first year in business, this will be zero. If this is not your first year in business, this amount will be the amount from Line 41 of your previous year's Schedule C.

Line 36. Purchases less cost of items withdrawn for personal use. Let's break this down into two parts: 1) Purchases. That's easy. Simply add up the cost (at your wholesale cost, not the retail price you intend to sell it at) of all your product which was bought during the year. If you didn't use any of these products yourself, you're done. Just put that amount on Line 36. But if you did happen to take some of your product and use it for yourself, then the second part of this description comes into play: 2) less cost of items withdrawn for personal use. If you have any product that was withdrawn for personal use, you must subtract that amount from the total amount of product purchased and enter the difference on Line 36.

Line 37-39. Most Sole Proprietors who sell product don't have anything on these 4 lines. These lines are typically used by manufacturers who must report the cost of labor expense (Line 37), Materials and supplies (Line 38), and Other costs (Line 39) directly related to the manufacture of their product. If you are not a manufacturer, just ignore these 3 lines.

Line 40. Add lines 35 through 39. Yup, just do what it says. This will give you the total of all your product costs.

Line 41. This is your ending inventory. Add up the cost (again, at your wholesale cost, not the retail price your customers pay you) of all unsold product on hand at the end of the year.

Line 42. Cost of goods sold. You simply subtract Line 41 from Line 40 and Voila! You've calculate the cost of the product actually sold during the year. Now take this Line 42 amount and transfer it to Line 4.

Chapter 29. How to Prepare Schedule C, Lines 43-47

If you are a Sole Proprietor who is deducting Car and truck expenses on Schedule C, Line 9, you may be required to complete Part IV of Schedule C, "Information on Your Vehicle." The purpose of this article is to explain how to complete this section of Schedule C.

Schedule C, Part IV begins on Page 2, Line 43 and ends on Line 47. This is a series of information questions designed to find out more about the vehicle you used for business. Here's an explanation of each line in this section.

Line 43. When did you place your vehicle in service for business purposes? Answer this question with the month, day and year that your first used your vehicle for the Sole Proprietorship.

Line 44. You must keep track of your mileage in order to answer this question. Here's what you must report: Total business miles (44a); Total commuting miles (44b); and Other miles (44c). In other words, you've got to keep track of the miles your drove the car for business purposes, as well as the miles you commuted to and from work (which is not a deductible business expense). The "Other" miles would be all personal miles other than commuting. The best way to have this mileage information available at the end of the year is to keep a mileage log.

Next comes a series of simple "Yes/No" questions:

Line 45. Was your vehicle available for personal use during off-duty hours? The answer to this is probably "yes". "Off-duty hours" means the time during the day when the car is not used for business purposes.

Line 46. Do you (or your spouse) have another vehicle available for personal use? Again, a very straightforward question. If you have another car (other than the one you drove for the business), the answer is "yes."

Line 47a. Do you have evidence to support your deduction? They are asking if you have written documentation of the mileage information provided on Line 44, such as a mileage log. Obviously, you want to be able to answer this question with a "yes."

Line 47b. If "Yes", is the evidence written? This appears to be a redundant question. If you answered 47a with a "yes," you have evidence to support your mileage deduction. And wouldn't it stand to reason that the evidence is written? What other kind of evidence would it be?

Chapter 30. Other Tax Forms That You May Be Required To File

All Sole Proprietors must prepare Schedule C as part of their federal personal income tax return. But it's likely that you can't stop there. As the old saying goes – "That's not all!" There's a pretty good chance that by filing a Schedule C, you must also file several other forms that are related to Schedule C. Here's a list of those forms and their relationship to Schedule C.

Schedule SE, Self-Employment Tax.

Go to Schedule C, Line 31. If you have a profit on this line of $400 or more (i.e. your income is greater than your expenses), you will also have to file Schedule SE in order to calculate your federal self-employment (SE) tax, aka the "dreaded" self-employment tax. SE tax is the sole proprietor's version of the employee's social security and medicare tax, which are automatically withheld from an employee's paycheck by the employer. You take the amount from Line 31 of Schedule C and transfer it to Schedule SE, Line 2.

Form 4562, Depreciation and Amortization.

If you purchased any equipment or other so-called "depreciable fixed assets" for use in your business, you may have to complete Form 4562 to report those purchases. "Depreciable fixed assets" include both personal property like computers and peripherals, printers, office furniture, office equipment such as fax machines and telephones, other business machinery, as well as real estate such as business buildings. The rules for filling out Form 4562 are quite complex and you'll definitely want to get some help here. (i.e. Don't try this at home!) The end result is that your total expense for purchasing business equipment is transferred from Form 4562 to Schedule C, Line 13, Depreciation and Section 179 expense.

Form 8829, Expenses for Business Use of Your Home.

The so-called "Home Office Expense" is one of the best tax breaks for the Sole Proprietor. But it doesn't come without jumping though some very specific recordkeeping hoops. To get this deduction, you must complete Form 8829 (or use the "Simplified Method" found on Schedule C, Line 30). Don't let the complexity of this form stop you, though. It could be well worth the time and effort. After doing From 8829, you transfer the amount from Line 35 (Allowable expenses for business use of your home) to Schedule C, Line 30.

For more on the Home Office deduction, go to the next chapter and read all about it!

CHAPTER 31. HOME OFFICE DEDUCTION

If you are a Sole Proprietor who wants to deduct your home office, you may want to file Form 8829, Expenses for Business Use of Your Home. The purpose of this chapter is to help you understand this form without getting a headache.

To keep things simple, this chapter also makes three assumptions about your business:

1. Your Sole Proprietorship is not an in-home daycare facility. If you happen to run that type of business, please consult a tax professional or the Form 8829 instructions.

2. Before taking the home office deduction, your business has a profit that is greater than your home office deduction. (The home office deduction cannot be used to create or increase a loss.)

3. You do not have any home casualty losses to deduct.

Here's a list of the information you need to properly complete Form 8829. After each item is the line on the form where that number is reported.

1. Square footage of your home office (Line 1)

2. Square footage of your entire home (Line 2)

3. Mortgage interest from Form 1098. Your lending institution is required to send you this by January 31. (Line 10)

4. Real estate taxes on your home (Line 11)

5. Homeowner's insurance premium. For both real estate taxes and homeowner's insurance, if you pay these as part of

THE PLAIN ENGLISH GUIDE TO 101 SELF-EMPLOYED TAX BREAKS

your monthly mortgage payment, these amounts should be reported on Form 1098. If you pay either the taxes or insurance yourself, then you'll need to track down those amounts in your checkbook register. (Line 17)

6. Rent payments, if you are renting rather than buying your home. (Line 18)

7. Repairs and maintenance expenses. This can include the typical expenses more homeowner's incur to keep their home in good shape, such as fixing a plumbing problem or repairing the water heater or furnace when they break down. Just be careful not to include major improvement projects like a new roof or bathroom remodel. Those are not considered repairs or maintenance. (Line 19)

8. Utilities expenses. This includes electricity, gas, water, sewer service, and trash disposal. It does not include telephone service. (Line 20)

9. Other expenses, such as neighborhood association dues and other miscellaneous household-related expenses not mentioned already. (Line 21)

After you put the square footage amount on Lines 1 and 2, you will divide Line 1 by Line 2 to calculate the business use percentage on Line 3. Then carry the Line 3 amount down to Line 7. This percentage is what determines how much of the various expenses will actually become a deductible business expense. For example, if you have a 150 square foot office and a 1,500 square foot home, your home office occupies 10% of your home and so you will get to deduct 10% of all the expenses listed above.

The next step is to list all those expenses on the various lines listed above, using column (b) Indirect expenses. Then you

SCHEDULE C TAX DEDUCTIONS REVEALED

add up all those expenses on Line 22 and then multiply that total by the business use percentage from Line 7, putting the result on Line 23. The Line 23 amount is then carried down to Line 35, and then you transfer the Line 35 amount to Schedule C, Line 30.

To calculate the depreciation expense on your home office, see the Form 8829 instructions for Part III, "Depreciation of Your Home."

One final note: Here's some potentially good news. The IRS now allows a second method for calculating the home office deduction that is significantly easier than the first method described above. It's called the "Simplified Method" and you'll find it right on Schedule C, Line 30. You multiply your home office square feet (up to 300) by $5. That's it! For details, check out the instructions for Schedule C or ask your accountant about it.

The potential disadvantage of the Simplified Method is obvious: you may get a smaller deduction than you would otherwise get by filing Form 8829.

By all means, calculate the deduction both ways and take whichever one gives you the larger deduction.

Chapter 32. 101 Deductions

Let's summarize what we've learned about taking deductions on Schedule C. We've covered a lot, and I'm glad you've read this far.

Perhaps your head is spinning like a top! Let's see if we can help you sort all this out by making one list of all the deductions we've covered, plus a few more that may not have been specifically mentioned in the book itself, but fall into one of the Schedule C expense categories.

There are actually more than 101 deductions here. The last time I counted, the list below has about 150 deductions (and counting). When I say, "There's 101 legal tax deductions for the self-employed," I'm speaking figuratively not literally.

The point is that regardless of the exact number, there are plenty of legal deductions for you to write off without any fear of an IRS audit.

Here they are, in the order they appear on Schedule C.

8-Advertising
Offline advertising
Print media space ads (yellow pages, etc.)
Coupon decks
Radio ads
TV ads
Press releases
Copywriting services
Sales Letters
Mailing lists

SCHEDULE C TAX DEDUCTIONS REVEALED

Newsletters
Brochures
Catalogues
Billboards
Birthday cards
Business cards
Trade shows, exhibits, displays
Graphics design
<u>Online advertising</u>
Website hosting services
Autoresponder services
Internet service provider
Email lists
Search engine optimization
Pay-per-click ads
Ezine ads
Banner ads
Affiliate program

9-Car & truck expenses

Gasoline
Oil
Repairs
Routine maintenance
Insurance
License plate fees
Registration
Auto club dues
Car loan interest
Lease expense
Property tax
Depreciation and/or Section 179 expense

THE PLAIN ENGLISH GUIDE TO 101 SELF-EMPLOYED TAX BREAKS

Parking
Tolls
Mileage
10-Commissions & Fees
Commissions
Fees
11-Contract Labor
12-Depletion
13-Business Equipment (Depreciation & Section 179)
Computer
Monitor
Printer
Telephone
Fax machine
Copier
Office furniture
Bookcase
File Cabinet
14-Employee benefits
Health insurance
Life Insurance
Dependent Care Assistance
Uniforms
Education reimbursement program
15-Insurance
Liability/malpractice insurance
Property insurance
Worker's compensation
16-Interest
Mortgage loan interest
Business credit card interest

Other commercial loan interest
17-Legal and professional services
Attorney fees
Auditing
Accounting services
Financial statement preparation
Billing services
Bookkeeping services
Tax return services (income tax)
Tax return services (payroll tax)
Tax return services (sales tax, property tax, etc.)
Tax representation
Payroll services
Tax Consulting services
Other Consulting services
18-Office expenses
Postage
Shipping
Paper/stationary
Folders
Staples, paper clips, writing utensils, etc.
19-Pension and profit-sharing plans
Employer contributions to retirement plans (SEP, SIMPLE, Keogh, 401k)
Administrative expenses
20-Rent or lease
Vehicle lease
Machinery rent
Equipment rent
Building rent
21-Repairs and maintenance

Repairs
Maintenance
Janitorial services
Landscaping
Lawn care
Security services
Trash removal
Exterminator services
22-Supplies
23-Taxes and licenses
Licenses
Personal property taxes
Real estate taxes
Fuel taxes
Sales taxes
Social security tax
Medicare tax
Federal unemployment tax
State unemployment tax
24a-Travel
Transportation
Lodging
Local transportation
Shipping
Laundry and dry cleaning
Phone calls
Tips
Meals (in travel status)
24b-Meals and entertainment
Meals (not in travel status)
Entertainment

SCHEDULE C TAX DEDUCTIONS REVEALED

25-Utilities
Electricity
Gas
Water
Sewer service
Trash disposal
Telephone (landline)
Telephone (cellular)

26-Wages
Hourly wages
Salary
Bonuses

27a-Other Expenses
Any other deductible business expenses not reported on lines 8-27a
Bad debt expense (accrual basis only)
Collections expense
Bank service charges
Safe deposit box
Dues/Memberships
Training & Education (seminars, conventions, etc.)
Books, magazines, trade journals (for your industry)
Books, magazines, newspapers (for customer waiting area)
Gifts (customers, employees, vendors, service providers)
Telephone

30-Home office deduction (business use of home)
Mortgage interest
Property taxes
Homeowner's insurance
Rent
Repairs

Maintenance
Utilities
Homeowner's association dues

Many Happy Returns!

Chapter 33. Now What?

Wondering what to do next? Here are 3 suggestions:

1. If you have questions about anything in this book, please take advantage of the free Tax Coupons I'm offering you.

To access the coupons immediately, visit www.selfemployedtaxdeductionstoday.com/tax-coupons.pdf

You'll get a 30-minute phone consultation with me, so you can pick my brain and get all your questions answered. You'll also receive a free confidential review of your most recently filed income tax return.

Altogether, this is a $150 value. It's is my way of saying "Thank you" for reading this book.

2. For 2 more free gifts, please visit www.SelfEmployedTaxDeductionsToday.com

You'll get instant access to my Special Report, "Top 10 Small Business Tax Deductions" as well as a subscription to my weekly Tax Newsletter.

3. Check my #1 Amazon Best-Selling Book, "Small Business Tax Deductions Revealed." This book explains tax reduction strategies that have saved my clients thousands of dollars. To get your copy today, Click Here or input this address into your internet browser:
http://www.amazon.com/dp/B00RW169CI

RECOMMENDED RESOURCES

This book is just the tip of the Tax World iceberg. There are many other excellent books on taxes for Small Business Owners and the Self-Employed. Here are three of my favorites.

Small Business Tax Deductions Revealed:
29 Tax-Saving Tips You Wish You Knew (For Self-Employed People Only)
Small Business Tax Tips, Volume 1
By Wayne Davies, EA (yes, I'm plugging my own book)
www.amazon.com/dp/B00RW169CI

Tired of paying so much tax to the IRS? You are not alone! Small business owners and self-employed people are overpaying their taxes by millions of dollars every year. "Small Business Tax Deductions Revealed" provides the tax reduction strategies you need to substantially lower your taxes. Read this book to discover "29 Tax-Saving Tips You Wish You Knew." These tax tips are perfectly legal self-employed tax deductions that you can use without any fear of the IRS.

Here you'll find the answers to questions like these:

What is the easiest way for a Small Business Owner/Self-Employed Person to lower your taxes? This tax strategy is so simple to understand and implement you'll be wondering why you haven't been using it for years.

Are you paying yourself the "right way" or the "wrong way"? Self-employed people are notorious for compensating themselves in a way that actually increases their taxes. Learn this tax tip and you'll know how to pay yourself so that you pay less tax, not more.

Do you know how to turn non-deductible personal medical expenses into a legitimate business expense? Most taxpayers can never write off medical expenses. This legal tax deduction changes all that.

How much money are you wasting on your retirement plan each year? There is a retirement plan for small business owners that will not cost you a dime, and enables you to contribute more than an IRA.

Do you know how to convert taxable income into tax-free income? Yes, it can be done. . . legally!

Are you deducting your commuting miles? Most business owners don't. "Small Business Tax Deductions Revealed" will show you how to do this without worrying about an audit. This tax deduction alone could save you a bundle.

Readers love the "plain English" writing style of author Wayne Davies. Imagine reading a book about self-employed tax deductions you can actually understand!

Here's what readers are saying:

"This book is clear and concise. It's as simple as tax talk can possibly be."

"I've never seen so much great tax info distilled into simple, even entertaining explanations."

THE PLAIN ENGLISH GUIDE TO 101 SELF-EMPLOYED TAX BREAKS

"No technical gobbledygook, just excellent information you can use immediately."

Looking for simple to follow, easy-to-understand explanations of our complex, mind-numbing tax laws? Would you like to have access to legal strategies than can reduce your small business and self-employment taxes? Then look no further than "Small Business Tax Deductions Revealed: 29 Tax-Saving Tips You Wish You Knew."

Small Business Taxes Made Easy:
How to Increase Your Deductions, Reduce What You Owe, and Boost Your Profits
By Eva Rosenberg, EA
www.amazon.com/dp/0071743278

In my opinion, Eva Rosenberg (aka "TaxMama") is the best Tax Teacher on the planet. She has not only written an excellent book on taxes for small business owners, she also runs a first-class website and newsletter, is a syndicated national columnist, and teaches tax professionals how to study for and pass the rigorous Enrolled Agent (EA) exam. I am one of her students. I took Eva's EA Exam Review course, and I would never have passed the EA exam with her help!

For more info about Eva and the many tax resources she offers, visit www.TaxMama.com

Here is my review of Eva's book "Small Business Taxes Made Easy."

"This book does exactly what it promises to do. Nothing could be more complicated that the wild and wacky world of business taxes. This book definitely makes understanding business taxes significantly easier. This is because Eva Rosenberg is a gifted teacher and writer -- she has the unique ability to take a complex subject and explain it in a way that makes sense. I've been reading Eva's articles and newsletter content for the past 7 years. I've attended her webinars and online classes. She really knows her stuff, and she takes what she knows and gives it to you in this book like she's sitting across the kitchen table and laying it all out for you.

So do not view the title and sub-title as marketing hype. If you own a small business or are thinking about starting one, or if you are self-employed or thinking about going solo, get this book and get a tax education you desperately need. You won't be disappointed. You will learn how to increase your deductions, reduce your taxes, and increase profits."

Lower Your Taxes - Big Time!
By Sanford Botkin, CPA
www.amazon.com/dp/0071849602

This is another great book. Here's my review.

"Sandy Botkin is one of America's top tax reduction specialists. I purchased a set of his audio CD's about 5 years ago on tax reduction strategies for small business owners and self-employed people and it was awesome. Well, he's managed to take virtually all the info from those CD's and put it in this book.

THE PLAIN ENGLISH GUIDE TO 101 SELF-EMPLOYED TAX BREAKS

This guy is a tax deduction machine-gun -- in rapid-fire manner, he spews forth one great tax-saving deduction after another. He used to work for the IRS as an auditor, and he's also a CPA, so he's one of the most knowledgeable tax experts I've ever encountered, and I've been preparing tax returns for a living for the past 20 years.

If you want to get your hands on practical tax-saving advice, get this book. I guarantee you'll find at least 10 or 20 or 30 (or more) tax deductions that you've never heard of before, or maybe you've heard about them but really didn't understand the finer points. Sandy will explain it all to you in an easy-to-understand writing style. He's a good communicator and has the knack for explaining difficult concepts in a way that non-accountants can understand."

About The Author

WAYNE M. DAVIES, EA has been doing individual and business tax returns for 25 years. He has personally prepared over 10,000 tax returns (and lived to tell about it).

Wayne specializes in providing tax reduction strategies to small business owners and the self-employed, including home-based business owners, freelancers, consultants and solo entrepreneurs.

For more of Wayne's tax-saving strategies, you can subscribe to his free small business Tax Newsletter at www.SelfEmployedTaxDeductionsToday.com

He also provides accounting and payroll services for all business types, as well as year-round tax planning.

You can contact Wayne at 260.480.7545 or via email at wayne.davies@supervalu.com

You can also connect with Wayne on Facebook at www.Facebook.com/GoodTaxPreparer

THE PLAIN ENGLISH GUIDE TO 101 SELF-EMPLOYED TAX BREAKS

ONE LAST THING...

If you enjoyed this book or found it useful I'd be very grateful if you'd post a short review on Amazon. Your support really does make a difference and I read all the reviews personally so I can get your feedback and make this book even better.

If you'd like to leave a review then please click below to visit the Amazon page for this book and scroll down to "Customer Reviews."

http://www.amazon.com/dp/B01AMB97SM/

Thanks again for your support!

Made in the USA
Las Vegas, NV
22 February 2024

86160961R00059